Original title:
The Frosted Horizon

Author: Jude Lancaster
ISBN HARDBACK: 978-9916-94-502-5
ISBN PAPERBACK: 978-9916-94-503-2

Glacial Echoes of Yesterday's Chill

In winter's grip, my socks did slide,
A frosty dance, I tried to hide.
But ice beneath my feet was swift,
I met the ground, oh what a gift!

A snowman grinned, all frosty white,
With carrot nose, he gave a fright.
I laughed so hard, I slipped once more,
He winked at me, I hit the floor!

The frozen birds in tree tops sang,
With icy notes, their humor rang.
I gave a cheer, they flapped in glee,
But landed right on my hot tea!

As icicles dripped with laughter's toll,
I dodged the frost, it took its toll.
Each moment bright with goofy fun,
In this cold world, I’m never done!

Beyond the Glacial Edge

Penguins dance in their tuxedos,
Waddle wiggling, pointing toes,
Icebergs melt with a grin so wide,
While seals laugh, trying to hide.

Snowmen start a snowball fight,
Carrots fly with all their might,
A polar bear just shakes his head,
"Chill out guys, let's go to bed!"

Silver Lining over a Frosted Plain

A squirrel went to track its nuts,
But slipped and fell into some cuts,
He rolled away, a fuzzy mess,
Chasing dreams of warmth, no less.

Frosty flakes upon a chair,
Kids slide down, they squeal and flare,
The dogs bark back, they join the spree,
Both tripping over joy, you see!

A Symphony of Snowy Silence

Winter’s quiet, or so they say,
But icicles drip and find their way,
A curious crow starts to caw,
"Yo, it's cold—seriously, raw!"

The trees are dressed in white and fluff,
Yet they look like they’ve had enough,
With branches bent and snowy feet,
They shuffle around and try to greet.

Frost-Bound Dreams of Dusk

Chill winds howl like a hungry ghost,
While the snowflakes gather, make the most,
Of frigid nights with dreams of cheese,
As mice play tag with such great ease.

Under blankets, snug like bugs,
Hot cocoa’s warm with marshmallow hugs,
Inside, the world is jam-packed cheer,
While outside, snowman sneezes near!

The Shimmering Edge of Dusk

As daylight fades and shadows creep,
Imaginary penguins start to leap.
They waddle and twirl in a frosty parade,
Chasing snowflakes that dance and evade.

Squirrels in sweaters throw snowball fights,
While snowmen wear sunglasses on chilly nights.
A silly ballet of winter delight,
As giggles echo ‘neath the twilight light.

Hushed Footsteps on Snowy Paths

In the silence, a crunch underfoot,
A squirrel giggles, forgetting his loot.
He slips on ice, takes a tumble and rolls,
Chasing his nuts with comical strolls.

Feel the chill, but don't lose your shoe,
A snowman grins, with a carrot or two.
He offers hot cocoa with a frosty grin,
But beware his hat, it might just spin!

Echoes of a Candlelit Hearth

With candles aglow, the shadows dance,
But wait—am I seeing a snowman prance?
He’s jitterbugging near the marshmallow stash,
While grandma’s knitting unravels in a flash!

The cats are plotting behind the chair’s rise,
Dreaming of biscuits and wintertime pies.
The fire crackles, a jolly faint cheer,
While we all giggle, sipping spiced beer!

When Frost Kisses the Earth

Outside, the world shines like a bright mint treat,
But watch out for that frostbite on your feet!
A cat in a scarf leaps with a frown,
As he skids on ice, then tumbles down.

In the morning glow, the sun starts to peek,
Snowflakes shimmer, oh so unique!
But imagine the snowman wearing a hat,
Who dreams of summer and a sunny chat.

Whispers of Winter's Embrace

Snowflakes tumble down with flair,
They dance like folks without a care.
Socks on the line, a frozen sight,
The dog may slip, oh what a fright!

Kids roll snowmen, round and wide,
One had a carrot, but it just cried!
Here comes a snowball, aimed too tight,
Hit the dad and what a flight!

Winter's laughter, loud and clear,
As icicles dangle, sharp and sheer.
The tea is hot, it fills the room,
While outside, squirrels plot their gloom.

But with each sip, we toast to cheer,
No frost will freeze our silly jeers.
With warm mittens on, we’ll not feel shy,
Let’s build a snow fort, reach for the sky!

Glacial Dreams at Dawn

Morning breaks with frosty breath,
The world’s a canvas, still as death.
Yet here comes a penguin in a tie,
Sliding past with a wink and a sigh.

The coffee pot sings, all steamy and bright,
While snow men gossip, what a sight!
A snowball fight breaks out with glee,
Watch your back, or you might be free!

Birds wear hats, who knew they would?
Flapping by, as if they could.
The sun peeks out, a yellow crown,
Under its glow, the grumpies drown.

So raise your mugs to winter’s cheer,
With snowflakes drifting, do not fear.
Let’s dance in boots and spin around,
For glacial dreams in joy abound!

Chilling Echoes of Morning Light

A squirrel sings in icy trees,
With tunes that float upon the breeze.
His whiskers frozen, yet so spry,
He swings from branches, oh my, oh my!

The snowflakes whisper tales of yore,
Of grumpy cats and open doors.
Hot cocoa spills and marshmallows hop,
A fluffy challenge — we can’t stop!

Bright colors clash against the white,
A fashion statement, what a sight!
Fuzzy earmuffs with polka dots,
Who says winter must have its knots?

So gather ‘round for giggles and fun,
With chilly air and warming sun.
For laughter echoes, light as air,
In every frosted, playful tear!

Beneath the Silver Shroud

Beneath a blanket, soft and bold,
Lies a world where stories unfold.
With snowmen watching from afar,
And penguins dreaming under stars.

The porcupine prances with a grin,
Waddling joyously, I dare him spin!
A flake lands gently on his nose,
With a sneeze so loud, the whole world knows.

Snow-covered bushes hold secrets tight,
While a rabbit hops in pure delight.
Chasing shadows, slipping low,
He trips and rolls—what a wacky show!

So here’s to laughter in frosty lanes,
Where winter’s magic sings in chains.
Let’s spin and twirl with silly delight,
For beneath the silver, things feel just right!

Frosted Vistas of a Silent World

Snowflakes fall with a giggle,
They dance like stars on a wiggle.
A snowman grins with a carrot nose,
Wearing socks that mismatched, who knows?

Chill winds tease the frosty trees,
Whispering jokes with a shimmered breeze.
Sleds go racing, oh what a sight,
Falling down, they giggle with delight.

Icicles hang like pointy hats,
While penguins waddle, they're sheer brats.
Snowball fights in a flurry panache,
Who's the winner? Well, that's just a laugh!

Each white wonder brings glee anew,
As snowmen plot their frosty coup.
So gather 'round this chilly spree,
For laughter's warmth is the key to glee!

Silhouettes in a Crystal Grove

Under bows that shimmer and glare,
Elves in scarves dance without a care.
They trip on frost like it’s a game,
Spreading giggles while swaying the same.

Snowflakes tickle their noses bright,
As they laugh in the pale moonlight.
Twinkling shadows twirl and spin,
In this grove where silliness begins.

Branches bow from the weight of snow,
Dropping flakes in a playful flow.
Bunnies leap in a frosty show,
Slipping and sliding in joyous throes.

Each turn brings a grin so wide,
With winter's antics, there’s no need to hide.
As the night sparkles with laughter's glow,
In this crystal grove, the fun’s on show!

Tales Woven in Ice and Air

Beneath the quilt of chill and gleam,
Frosty tales flow like a wacky dream.
A dragon made of snowflakes flies,
Chasing snowflakes that tickle the skies.

Here, the rabbits wear hats so bright,
With scarves that swirl in pure delight.
Their antics draw a crowd of cheer,
As laughter echoes for all to hear.

Frozen lakes are odes of joy,
Where penguins surf like every toy.
With every slide and icy crash,
The giggles ring out with a splashing splash.

So gather 'round, let stories unfold,
In this frosty realm that never grows old.
For laughter's the art in this frosty fair,
In this whimsical world, there’s joy to share!

Twilight's Breath on a Frozen Lake

As twilight throws a chilly stare,
The lake dons its crystal, frosty wear.
Skates glide along like ducks on a spree,
With slip-ups met by shouts of glee.

Snowflakes whisper jokes in the chill,
While skiers carve down the icy hill.
A seal wearing shades makes a dash,
In this frozen realm where fun’s a splash.

Friends bundled tight in colorful gear,
Making snow forts while sharing a cheer.
With hot cocoa warming tiny hands,
They revel in laughter across icy lands.

Twilight's breath brings a giggling sound,
As the frozen lake bounces joy all around.
So join the fun, don’t miss a beat,
In this frosty realm where laughter's a treat!

The Quietude of Frigid Twilight

Snowflakes dance with silly grace,
As winter squirrels race for space.
A penguin slips, lands on its back,
While laughing at a snowman’s snack.

Two rabbits gossip, tails in swirl,
One says, 'Have you seen that girl?'
The other nods with frosty glee,
Then tumbles down a frosty tree.

Icicles jingle like tiny bells,
As frosty owls spread comical yells.
They argue over who’s more wise,
But both get lost beneath the skies.

Amidst the quiet, giggles seep,
While snowmen dream of warm, soft sheep.
They ponder jokes of winter's plight,
And share their laughs in the pale light.

Enchanted by the Gleaming Chill

A polar bear in shades so bright,
Struts around, a chilly sight.
With sunglasses on, he takes a seat,
Munching on his frosty treat.

The penguins waddle, fancy-free,
In feathered hats for all to see.
They glide on ice, a comical sight,
While trying hard to stay upright.

A snowman boasts of frosty fame,
'They've named a blizzard after my name!'
Then stumbles as the winds grow bold,
And falls in snow, a sight to behold!

As ice crystals twinkle in moon's glare,
Laughter echoes through the chilly air.
Winter's antics never cease,
Creating joy and silly peace.

Ethereal Paths in a Frosty Realm

A rabbit in boots hops on the snow,
'This isn't so bad, you know!'
It starts a jig, a frosty prance,
While dodgeball snowballs give it a chance.

The trees wear coats of icy lace,
As giggling children join the race.
One slips, falls, then starts to roll,
Creating a snow angel in a bowl.

Frosty balloons float across the way,
They bounce around, come out to play.
With laughter loud, the night ignites,
As snowflakes twirl in festive flights.

Winter's whimsy fills the night,
With shining stars and sheer delight.
In this frosty, funny dance,
Life is joyful with a chance.

Shards of Serenity Where Shadows Play

A cat in boots stalks snowflakes high,
With a pounce so bold, it gives a cry.
It swats at shadows with much grace,
Missing them all, what a silly chase!

Snowmen argue of who's more round,
While twirling their carrot noses around.
'I've got a hat from a lovely store!'
'But I've got a top hat and so much more!'

Birds in beanies chirp a tune,
While a tiny mouse croons to the moon.
They share a laugh, a comical crowd,
As snowflakes swirl and gather loud.

In the silent Narnia of white,
Mirth dances with the soft moonlight.
Joy reigns where cold winds blow,
In frosty realms where laughter grows.

Frost and Fire on the Northern Skyline

In the morning light so bright,
Snowflakes dance in pure delight.
An icy breeze gives me a chill,
I sip my coffee, feel the thrill.

A penguin winked, what a sight!
It skated by, oh what a fright!
With every slip and every slide,
I laughed so hard, I nearly cried.

The sun pops up, what a tease,
Melting snow with such great ease.
A sizzling snowman starts to pout,
"Why's it so hot? I'm out! I'm out!"

But bulbs of frost twinkle late,
Doing the disco, feeling great.
With chilly prance, they gleefully sing,
Life’s a freeze, let’s dance, let’s swing!

Luminous Traces of a Frozen Canvas

In the night, the moon does glow,
Painting silver on the snow.
A snowflake lands atop my nose,
It tickles me, oh how it goes!

With laughter echoing so clear,
Frosty friends all gather near.
We build a snowman, round and stout,
He shouts, "I'm cool! Let’s throw a clout!"

Painting stars with chilly flair,
It’s a masterpiece beyond compare.
Frosty brush strokes in the air,
The universe must really care!

A rabbit hops to take a look,
Scribbling snow like a storybook.
With every leap and frosty hop,
We're jesters beneath the frozen top!

When Icy Fingers Paint the Sky

I look up high to see what’s there,
A dancing cloud that’s full of flair.
It tickles the sun, a playful tease,
While frosty fingers wave with ease.

A playful snowball flies right by,
It hits a squirrel, oh my oh my!
He shakes it off, with furry pride,
Scurrying off, he runs to hide.

Icicles dangle, a crystal show,
Catch them quick, you’ll never know.
One might fall and that’ll be fun,
Watch out, they’re heavy, run, run, run!

Dancing flakes, a colorful spree,
A circus act for all to see.
With giggles loud and spirits high,
When icy fingers paint the sky!

The Frosted Edge of Tomorrow

The dawn breaks with a frosty grin,
Snowflakes whirl like they're in a spin.
I slip and slide, a total mess,
But joy finds me in this winter dress.

Tomorrow’s chill is here to stay,
I giggle as I tumble, hooray!
Each frosty patch a surprise awaits,
Yet warmth abounds in playful fates.

Frosted donuts, round and sweet,
Who’d have thought this snowy treat?
With sprinkles red, looking all fine,
Winter’s joy is truly divine!

So here’s to frost and laughter bold,
Winter’s secrets waiting to unfold.
With a spring in our just-icy feet,
Life’s more fun with snow and sleet!

The Glimmering Veil of Nightfall

When night does fall, with a twinkly grin,
The stars come out, like they've lost a bet.
A raccoon dines well, in the moonlight's glow,
Is he the king? Oh, you can bet!

The shadows dance, playing hide and seek,
While owls hoot jokes, that make you snort.
The wind whispers secrets, all quite unique,
As squirrels debate their winter sport!

The moon's a spotlight, on this funny stage,
Where snowflakes prance, with a fluttering flair.
A penguin in pajamas, could steal the wage,
Of any comedian, if he dared!

So here we laugh, at the frost's delight,
With sparkles of joy, and a chill in the air.
Who knew that winter could be such a sight?
In this frozen world, we'll dance without care!

A Canvas of White and Wonder

Blankets of white, spread like buttercream,
Snowmen stand tall, with a carrot up top.
One winks at you, it’s a snowy daydream,
While snowflakes twirl, and the little kids hop.

A blizzard rolls in, like a strange doughnut,
Chasing the sleds as they zoom down the hill.
The dog’s in the lead, getting stuck in a rut,
While chasing his tail with unmatched thrill!

Snowball fights break out, with the joy of a child,
While someone gets pelted, with laughter so loud.
“Is that your aim?” one cackles, all but reviled,
As they point to the snowman who’s laughing out loud.

We dance in the flurry, rolling snowballs tight,
Creating pure magic, in a whirling delight.
With giggles, and joy, the fun feels so right,
In this winter wonderland, we take flight!

Secrets Beneath the Icy Expanse

Under the ice, where the fish debate,
Turtle wears shades, says he's seen it all.
“I got a great deal, catch you all a plate,”
But the catfish snickers, as he starts to brawl.

Seals have a party, with umbrellas in hand,
Throwing a bash, on an iceberg so high.
Dancing to tunes, while the walruses plan,
Outfitting the igloos for a snowball fight!

An octopus juggles, while fish take the stage,
Mermaids are laughing, as they shoot for the moon.
“Did you hear that joke?” they beckon—“So sage!”
And amid the chuckles, they burst into tune.

What secrets they share, in a world so vast,
With a chuckle of ice, and a wink at the sun.
So come take a peek, where the wild times are cast,
Beneath the cool surface, oh what fun has begun!

Frozen Secrets of the Setting Sun

When the sun dips low, painting skies ablaze,
Snowmen conspire, brewing mischief and cheer.
A flock of pink flamingos, lost in a maze,
Wonder if winter coats would make them less clear.

The shadows retreat, as much as they can,
Biting remarks from a cheeky old crow.
“Why don’t you stay? You could pass for a fan,
And I could use someone to tell me a joke!”

Hats made of snow sit atop frosty heads,
Each one a character, with quirks of their own.
Chortles abound as the laughter spreads,
While the sun dips low, turning day into clone.

So we gather ‘round as the night takes its cue,
With warm cups of cocoa, and jesters to spare.
In this frozen realm, where adventure is true,
The secrets we find in the chill of the air!

Echoes in a Shimmering Void

In a land where ice cubes roam free,
A penguin rides a scooter with glee.
Snowmen debate about carrot cuisine,
While a frosty cat juggles a tangerine.

Hockey pucks skate across frozen lakes,
As polar bears bake up yummy cakes.
Jack Frost claims he’s a chill superstar,
With his icy jokes, they never go far.

The snowflakes giggle, twirl in the air,
A chilly ballet, oh what a flair!
They land on a squirrel, who’s lost in thought,
Wondering if snowball fights can be bought.

So let’s raise our mittens to this cute scene,
Where winter’s absurdity reigns like a queen.
For laughter wraps tightly in frost’s embrace,
As we dance round the ice in a comical race.

Glacial Reflections in the Stillness

A frozen lake turned into a stage,
Where walruses dance, like a funny mage.
Chill winds whistle a tune, quite absurd,
While a seal tries hard not to be heard.

Snowflakes debate if they're just puffs of air,
While igloos are dressed with the latest flair.
A polar bear tiptoes, looking so sly,
Chasing a snowmobile pie in the sky.

Icicles hang like bells on a tree,
As a frosty fox sings in harmony.
He thinks he's a bard with his icy replies,
While frosty mimosas vaporize lies.

So here in this glacial, quirky affair,
We cheer for the weirdness that's found everywhere.
With snorts and giggles amid chilly sights,
We embrace all the joy of frostbitten nights.

Frosty Whispers of Olde

In a realm where the snowflakes knit tales,
A grandpa reindeer tells jokes with big gales.
He chuckles so hard, his antlers all jiggle,
As penguins play tag with a flickering wiggle.

The icebergs hold secrets of feathery whim,
While a chilly squirrel puts on a grim grin.
He claims that his acorns are hats on his head,
While nesting on ice that's perfectly spread.

A snowy owl hoots, "I'm a scholar of frost,"
Yet misplaced his glasses, oh what a cost!
He searches for knowledge beneath frosty crowns,
While a dancing snow hare wears glittery gowns.

So gather your mittens and join in the fun,
In this world of frost where the laughter's begun.
With whimsy and wonder, we'll waddle along,
To the beat of the frost, and sing winter's song.

Hues of Twilight in Frosty Gleam

Under twilight's glow, the frost starts to play,
As llamas in hats decide to sashay.
They twirl and they spin, their wool fuzzy bright,
While frosty skates glisten in twilight delight.

A moose with a scarf does a jig on the ice,
Claiming his moves are both graceful and nice.
The fish in the pond chuckle high from below,
As he slips on a patch—what a comical show!

The trees wear white sparkles, like glitter in cheer,
As owls throw a party, inviting all near.
With snacks made of snow and drinks made of freeze,
Winter’s gathering brings giggles with ease.

So let’s toast the twilight, with humor and flair,
For laughter rings brightly in the frozen air.
In this world of chill, where the funny takes flight,
We’ll revel in joy till the morning’s first light.

Beneath the Stillness of Frozen Time

Icicles hang like candy canes,
Snowmen wobble in silly strains.
Penguins ice skate, full of flair,
While squirrels debate who's the best pair.

Footprints lead to nowhere fast,
Someone slipped, now they won't last.
Jacket zippers stuck like glue,
And hot cocoa fights, oh what a brew!

Frosty cheeks and noses red,
Hot dogs wearing hats instead.
Huddled close, we laugh and cheer,
Winter's antics draw us near.

In snowball battles, no one's safe,
Each throw lands with a goofy waif.
But beneath this frosty show,
Laughter blooms where warmth can grow.

Dreaming in a Frosted Reverie

A snowy dreamscape, oh so bright,
Ice cream cones, in a strange delight.
Bunny slippers skip and hop,
While marshmallows dance, they just won’t stop.

Frosty breath in the chilly air,
I swear those snowflakes want to share.
With winter hats, we start to twirl,
As penguins prank and give a whirl.

In cozy corners, cocoa spills,
As chocolate chips, they do high drills.
With a sprinkle here, a giggle there,
The world becomes a frosty fair.

Tangled scarves and mismatched boots,
Sledding down on hilly hoots.
What a sight, this snowy spree,
Dreaming of warmth, oh let it be!

Where Light Meets Icy Depths

A shiny ball, it rolls away,
It hits the dog—he's had his play!
The sun’s a trickster on this day,
Reflecting off in a frosty sway.

Fingers numb, we grip the gear,
As snowflakes gather, oh so near.
Frogs wearing hats, oh what a sight,
They croak along in sheer delight.

Snowy owls dressed in formal wear,
Giggling freely without a care.
A dance-off starts, just look at them go,
Who knew frozen fun could steal the show?

Kites made of snowflakes take to flight,
While we toast marshmallows with all our might.
Where shadows frolic, laughter escapes,
In this frosted world, it’s all great shapes.

The Shimmering Path of Winter's Journey

Snowplows rumble like monsters bold,
They chase away what feels like cold.
Chickens cluck in feathered suits,
While raccoons gossip about new boots.

With candy cane sticks, we march in line,
Hiking on trails, that seem divine.
Banana peels on a frosty slope,
Watch your step, just keep your hope!

A blizzard comes, it's full of flair,
But we invent games without a care.
Snowflakes whisper funny things,
Wheeling in laughter, winter brings!

In snow many colors, a palette bright,
We paint our joy, and hold on tight.
With friends and giggles, we own this quest,
Wander the path, snowball wars—our zest!

The Glinted Path of Winter's Heart

Snowflakes dance like playful sprites,
The ground's a slippery playground at night.
Careful now, don't lose your style,
Or channel your inner penguin for a while.

Icicles hang like frozen swords,
Watch out! They're nature's pointy hoards.
Laughter trails as we take a fall,
But hey, at least we won't feel small!

Hot cocoa warms our chilly hands,
Marshmallows float like cottony lands.
We sip our drinks and make a toast,
To winter wonders, we love the most!

So grab your sled, let's slip and slide,
A snowy joy ride, a frosty glide.
In every tumble, there's delight,
As winter laughs, we're light as light!

A Soft Whisper in the Chill

A whisper blows through the frosty trees,
Reminding us of coldest knees.
Socks are soggy, hats a bit snug,
Winter's here, so give a tug!

Snowmen pop up, grinning wide,
With carrot noses, arms outstretched wide.
Until a kid runs, gives a shove,
What a sad way to show some love!

Footprints lead in a zigzag race,
One slip, and down goes the face!
Chasing friends, we make a pact,
No laughing at that awkward act!

Yet, there's magic in this frosty air,
Laughter echoes everywhere.
A moment shared, a frosted grin,
With every drift, let the fun begin!

Under the Gaze of Icy Stars

Stars twinkle bright in the frozen sky,
Wishing on them seems a little sly.
Santa’s sleigh takes a nosedive,
‘Cause Rudolph's tired of this jive!

Snowflakes tumble like clumsy dreams,
Caught in the wind, or so it seems.
Can we catch one on our tongue?
A frosty surprise that’s oh so fun!

Fireside tales with a marshmallow roast,
We're the winter's wacky host.
S’mores with giggles echo the night,
In this chilly world, we find delight!

Each icy breath brings a laugh so bold,
In the magic of winter, we feel the gold.
A dance through the snow, we twirl and glide,
With icy stars, our hearts collide!

The Stillness of Shivering Memories

Memories freeze on a winter day,
Like leftovers packed for a long stay.
Grandma's quilt wraps us in snug,
Listening to stories with a winter hug!

Snow forts built with teamwork schemes,
By the evening, we're tired from dreams.
But look! A snowball aimed in jest,
To dodge or catch? A winter test!

Twinkling lights on every house,
Mice made of snow ignite the rouse.
But next morning, the mouse fights back,
And our boots, oh no! They're under attack!

Through laughter shared and silly slips,
We embrace the freeze with joyful quips.
In the stillness, our hearts beat loud,
Winter's frosty, but we're so proud!

A Dance of Shadows and Snowflakes

Snowflakes tumble, do a jig,
Shadows peak, then laugh so big.
They spin and swirl with frozen grace,
Chasing each other, in this space.

A snowman winks with a carrot nose,
While snowballs fly, oh, how it goes!
Frosty friends with hats askew,
In this frosty dance, our laughter grew.

But watch your step, oh, slippery ground,
One quick twirl, and you'll be down!
The snowflakes giggle, a merry sight,
Life's just better in winter’s light!

As shadows creep and sun goes down,
We can't help but laugh, not frown.
In this chill of winter's spree,
The dance goes on, just you and me.

The Stillness of Cold Blue Hours

Stars blink down, a chilly wink,
Someone's dog just took a drink.
In this stillness, giggles wake,
As someone slips on icy flake.

The moon’s all round, like a snowball bright,
While penguins march, taking flight.
They slip and slide in glittered frost,
In this hour, a winter’s cost!

Cold blue shadows dance around,
As fallen snowflakes touch the ground.
But laughter erupts, a joyful sound,
In blue hours, happiness found.

So warm your heart in frosty air,
With laughter bright, and snowy flair.
A quiet moment that feels so fine,
Under stars that glitter and shine.

Unraveled by the Icebound Gaze

In winter's grip, a frozen stare,
We bundled up, a stylish pair.
But on the ice, we slip and slide,
While polar bears laugh with pride.

A snowman’s hat flies off in glee,
Chasing after, oh, look at me!
With frosty breath and cheeks like rose,
We tumble down, and laughter flows.

Glittered landscapes, a pristine lace,
As squirrels plot a nutty chase.
Those furry friends with dashing flair,
In this frozen world, we share a scare!

But what’s a trip without some fun?
We shake it off and run, run, run!
In the glisten of a snowy daze,
We all unwind with frozen gaze.

Celestial Glare on Winterscape

The sun peeks out, a cheeky grin,
With snowflakes twinkling like a violin.
While penguins waltz, with dignity cold,
Winter’s stage, a sight to behold!

A little bird hops and sings,
Wearing a scarf—oh, what fun that brings!
While ice skaters spin with delight,
Their pirouettes a silly sight.

In this landscape of dazzling glare,
Snowmen challenge us, unaware.
“Bet you can’t catch us!” they tease and jest,
But we find joy in a frozen quest!

So laugh aloud in this frosty place,
As winter dances, a charming race.
With every slip, and every cheer,
The celestial glare brings us near.

The Dance of Frozen Whispers

In winter's chill, the socks do slide,
The snowman wobbles, he’s quite a glide.
Penguins in tuxes, oh what a sight,
Dance on the ice till the morning light.

Hot cocoa spills, marshmallows fly,
Sipping from mugs, we laugh and sigh.
The icicles dangle, a silly show,
Pointy hats on snowmen, oh no, oh no!

A squirrel in boots, just struts with flair,
Chasing its tail, without a care.
Frosty the snowman, he lost his nose,
Replaced it with carrots, he giggles and goes.

So let’s make mischief, let laughter ring,
In this frozen world, it’s a silly thing!
With frosty whispers that giggle and tease,
Let’s twirl and swirl in the winter breeze!

Celestial Gleam of Winter’s Breath

Stars twinkle brightly on blankets of snow,
As reindeer attempt a comical show.
Falling like snowflakes, they tumble and roll,
Noses collide with a cheeky goal.

Sledding down hills, giggles abound,
Who knew that snowballs were round and profound?
Frostbite might sting, oh what a pain,
But laughter rings out, like a joyful refrain.

The moon smiles wide, sharing secrets with trees,
While frostbitten fingers beg for some cheese.
Snow forts are built with great care and thought,
Pending attack from the snowballish lot!

So grab your mittens and dash to the street,
Winter’s a playground where summer’s a cheat!
With dreams in our pockets, we’ll shimmy and sway,
As moonlight dances in a frosty ballet.

Crystalline Secrets in the Air

A snowflake's secret, it giggles and spins,
Making snow angels with frosty grins.
Laughter erupts from the frozen ground,
As jackets get stuck, with a funny sound.

Ice creams of snow, they melt in the sun,
Sipping on slush, oh what frozen fun!
Rabbits in scarves prance in delight,
Bonkers bunnies hop into the night.

Frostbitten noses, faces aglow,
Catch a few snowflakes as they softly flow.
With shivers and quivers, we dash through the park,
Wishing for summer while singing till dark.

So let's laugh at winter, at slides and spills,
Through snowball fights and frosty thrills.
A crystalline wonderland, oh what a sight,
Where giggles and ice make everything bright!

A Tapestry of Frost and Silence

In the morn, everything’s wrapped in white,
I tripped on my boot, oh what a sight!
The cat on a sled, it zooms with flair,
While I’m stuck giggling, lost in mid-air.

Breezes whisper secrets of past snowy days,
Building snow forts in a thousand ways.
Hot chocolate fountains, they've run amok,
The marshmallows float like ships in a dock.

The frost paints pictures on windows clear,
While snowflakes do ballet, oh how they cheer!
A penguin with glasses, doing math with flair,
Proclaims that a snowstorm is “fashioned with care.”

As the sun sets low, it giggles in glow,
Sharing its warmth with a soft, mellow show.
In this frozen tapestry, all laughter's alive,
Snowmen just chuckle, as we all take a dive!

Frosted Dawn's Embrace

Morning light does twist and twirl,
Snowflakes prance and give a whirl.
Coffee cups are warm with cheer,
As winter's giggles fill the air.

Frosty breath goes up, then down,
Like a clown, I stalk the town.
Slipping, sliding on the way,
Making snowmen lead the play.

Carrots noses, eyes of coal,
These silly figures take a stroll.
Snowballs fly, laughter rings loud,
Winter's joy, our silly cloud.

Under blankets, snuggled tight,
Dreaming of our snowy flight.
In this chill, we find the fun,
As frosty giggles have begun.

Where Snowflakes Dance at Dusk

Gather round as evening falls,
Snowflakes come to make their calls.
Each a twirl, each a spin,
Dancing 'round, let the games begin!

With a whoosh and a little squeak,
I'll build a fort, so unique.
But snowmen laugh when they just fall,
It's a chilly, giggly brawl!

Laughter echoes through the night,
As we chase flurries in moonlight.
Frosty boots and scarves askew,
Who knew winter could be so goo?

As dusk wraps up the snowy day,
We stumble home, lost in play.
With rosy cheeks and hearts that leap,
In this frosty world, we just don't sleep!

Secrets Beneath the Ice

Underneath the frosty glaze,
Whispers hide in frosty bays.
Skating past with chosen flair,
Twisting like we just don't care.

Icebergs float, with secrets grand,
As penguins waddle, hand in hand.
Who knew that ice could hold such glee?
Like a show on ice, lucky me!

Gliding smooth like butter spread,
Only to fall, oh what a dread!
Laughter bubbles in the fray,
As winter's stunts lead us astray.

So tiptoe on this frozen stage,
Where giggles turn to winter's page.
With each slip, another tale,
In every frosty, cheerful gale!

Glimmering Silence of Twilight

As twilight paints the snowy ground,
In silence, giggles can be found.
Frosted whispers, secrets near,
Crafting snowflakes with good cheer.

A snowball fight, oh what a blast,
With fluffy flurries flying fast!
Who knew cold could feel so bright?
Each throw’s a spark, a silly sight.

Twilight glimmers, stars ignite,
Winter’s magic feels just right.
In this hush, our laughter swells,
Tales of snow are what winter tells.

With each glide, our spirits soar,
Slipping, tumbling, who could ask for more?
In this glowing, wintry bite,
We find the fun in winter’s light!

A Glacial Heartbeat in Stillness

In winter's chill, my heart does quake,
Each snowflake falls, a funny mistake.
A penguin slips, then strikes a pose,
While I just laugh at frosty toes.

The icicles jingle like tiny bells,
As polar bears dance with frosty swells.
I trip on ice, and oh what joy,
A snowman winks at this clumsy girl!

With puffs of breath in the frosted air,
I challenge the snow to a snowball fair.
Yet every throw is met with a slide,
And laughter echoes, there's no place to hide.

So here I stand, not cold, but warm,
In laughter's light, I find my charm.
A glacial heartbeat, in stillness found,
Where joy and snowflakes swirl all around.

Crystalline Breath of an Arctic Night

Under the stars, the crystals gleam,
A scene so perfect, it feels like a dream.
I build a snowman, all tall and grand,
He tips his hat but can't understand.

As the cold moon laughs, it throws some light,
A squirrel in snow gear, what a sight!
With little ski poles, he tries to glide,
And faceplants hard, with winter pride.

Chasing snowflakes on frosty ground,
Falling and giggling, I spin around.
Each crystalline breath brings a chill of fun,
Those winter nights are far from done.

So raise a toast to the cold and bright,
Where chilly giggles take flight at night.
With every breath, a chuckle grows,
In the arctic's embrace, who knows what flows?

Snowbound Whispers in the Breeze

Whispers of snow dance with the breeze,
As penguins strut, aiming to please.
They slide and tumble in a flurry of white,
Oh, how they make this chill feel bright!

A frost-bitten cat takes a daring leap,
In a pile of snow, he's lost in deep sleep.
With snowflakes clinging to his furry cheek,
He dreams of summers, this furry sneak.

Laughter erupts as I trip once more,
My snowball fight's turned into a chore!
With red-nosed friends and chilly grins,
We roll 'round giggling till chaos begins.

Here snowbound whispers fill the air,
Each frosty breath, a joyful affair.
In a land where snowflakes fall with glee,
We craft our joy, wild and free!

The Lament of Frostbitten Leaves

Oh, leaves once green, now crisp and brown,
They rustle softly, in winter's gown.
A whispered cry from branches bare,
'We miss the sun!' they say in despair.

Frostbitten leaves in the chilly night,
They dream of summer, oh, what a sight!
Yet here they giggle, at their plight,
While squirrels dance in sheer delight.

Every breeze teases, makes them sway,
'Join our dance, don't fade away!'
As snowflakes cheer in a joyful play,
Those leaves are laughing, what a display!

So let us sing for the leaves of yore,
In winter's chill, they'll dance once more.
For in their laughter, we find relief,
In the frosty world of frostbitten leaves.

Shards of Glass in the Morning Light

Morning sun peeks through, so bright,
Windows wink, oh what a sight!
A squirrel slips on ice, oh dear,
Chasing breakfast, what a cheer!

Glittering shards on the ground,
Everywhere, they twinkle around.
A dog skids by, slips with a yelp,
A frosty dance, just like a kelp!

A mug of cocoa spills in haste,
Caught in laughter, we can't waste.
Laughter bubbles like a fountain,
On this frosty, icy mountain!

Winter's here with a playful grin,
We slip and slide, let the fun begin!
Shards of glass bring giggles galore,
In the morning light, we want more!

A Canvas of Crystal Dreams

Snowflakes twirl, a grand ballet,
Winter’s art on full display.
A snowman grins with a carrot nose,
Wearing my hat—everyone knows!

Kids with sleds fly down the hill,
Squeals of joy, the air so still.
But watch out for that bushy tree,
A crystal canvas, oh let it be!

A snowball whizzes, missed my head!
Laughter echoes, here's the dread.
Frosted dreams come to life today,
With giggles echoing in the fray!

Crisp air crackles, fills with delight,
Hot chocolate, oh, what a sight!
Winter wraps us in a warm embrace,
In this crystal dream, we find our place!

Echoes of the Frozen Sky

Looking up at a sky so clear,
A frozen poem, full of cheer.
Clouds whisper secrets, shy and sly,
While birds complain of being dry.

Icicles hang like daggers, oh no!
I slip and slide, the world’s a show.
Laughter rings out, the echo’s fun,
Underneath the chilling sun.

Snowmen giggle with frosty breath,
Our fumbles lead to winter's jest.
In this cold, we stumble and fall,
Every mishap a funny call!

As the frozen echoes fade away,
We’ll make more memories during the play.
With mirth and laughter, we ply our way,
This frosty journey we’ll forever stay!

Tranquil Radiance of the North

In the north where the chill resides,
Snowflakes dance on winter tides.
A penguin slips on glittered ice,
With frosty giggles, oh what a slice!

Glowing moonlight, shadows play,
We toss snowballs without delay.
A cat leaps out, oh what a sight,
Enchanted by moon's silver light!

A sled race starts, who will prevail?
We tumble down with a wailing wail.
Laughter echoes, bright and clear,
In this tranquil place, we know no fear!

With every fall and winter's cheer,
We slip and glide, our hearts sincere.
Radiant joy under starry veils,
In this frosty land, where laughter prevails!

Glints of Frost on Ocean's Breath

A penguin slid right off his boat,
Thought he was headed for a float.
But up he shot, quite like a dart,
Into the water—oh, that's smart!

The waves were cold, the frost was thick,
He blinked and swam, quite quick and slick.
The fish were laughing all around,
While he wore frost like a crown.

As seagulls quacked with gleeful glee,
He chirped back, 'Look, I'm fancy-free!'
With icy jewels that glimmer bright,
His chilly dance was quite a sight!

In frosty flair, he shimmied and rolled,
In this jolly game, he felt quite bold.
Who knew the ocean had such a twist?
This frolic on ice was not to miss!

Winter’s Soft Palette Unfurled

A snowman stood with a crooked hat,
He strutted around, the prince of that chat.
'I'm made of snow, fresh and cool,
But watch out for the kids at school!'

They came with snowballs, full of cheer,
'Let’s knock him down, have no fear!'
But he just giggled, snowflakes flew,
'Is that the best you've got, boo-hoo?'

With every throw, his arms went wide,
Instead of melting, he took it in stride.
'Come on, give me your best shot,
This winter’s chill is one hot pot!'

His laughter echoed through the trees,
A jolly sound on the icy breeze.
Turns out this winter, bright and gay,
Just means more fun come out and play!

Whispers of the Cold Moonlight

At midnight, raccoons danced on ice,
In their furry coats, they looked quite nice.
They twirled and spun in the pale moon's glow,
Tag-teaming fast, not moving slow.

'Who left this shine, this icy sheen?'
One raccoon said, with eyes agleam.
'It's a slippery stage made for our show,
Let’s impress the moon, it's our time to glow!'

They slipped and slid, what a sight to see!
A choreographed mess, yet so carefree.
With each fluffed tail and frantic leap,
They laughed and howled, not a peep from sleep.

The snowflakes fell, a twinkling delight,
As raccoons sang to the chill of night.
In moonlit revelry, they'd lose the frost,
For laughter shared is never lost!

Beneath the Shroud of Silver Frost

In the garden, things went awry,
Flowers froze, but oh my, oh my!
With petals stiff, they made a fuss,
'What’s next? A snowball fight for us?'

The daisies whispered, quite unfair,
While the tulips pouted, 'We need warm air!'
But then a rabbit hopped right in,
'Just chill out, friends, let the fun begin!'

He gathered pals, a motley crew,
Together they tossed the crisp and new.
Frosty petals flew high for flight,
And laughter bloomed, a pure delight!

So beneath frost, when moods run low,
Remember the joy that can still grow.
In every flake that twirls and spins,
Find the giggles where winter begins!

Translucent Dreams of a Frozen World

Snowflakes dance like tiny clowns,
Wearing coats of shimmering gowns.
They giggle as they tumble down,
Painting the world in a frosty frown.

Icicles hang like silly mustaches,
On roofs where the sunlight crashes.
They sparkle with a glint of cheer,
Making us question, 'How’d we get here?'

Snowmen grin with carrot noses,
Waving at passersby in poses.
But just wait till they start to melt,
You'll see the funny faces dealt!

Winter's here, oh what a jest,
Each snowflake makes a funny guest.
With every flurry, laughter flows,
In this frozen dreamland where silliness grows.

The Mirage of Winter’s Veil

A blanket white, like marshmallow fluff,
Parks turned to playgrounds, isn’t that tough?
Sleds racing down with a squeal of delight,
While mittens disappear, oh what a sight!

Frosted trees wear shimmering coats,
While snowball fights bring out playful gloat.
Snowmen hold court on a chilly stage,
As winter plays tricks, what's all the rage?

Penguins slide like they own the scene,
In a world so white, like a dream machine.
They waddle and tumble, fall on their backs,
Claiming victory in their fluffy tracks!

Through swirling flakes, a mirthful show,
As winter's veil begins to glow.
With every giggle, the chill subsides,
In this funny place where joy abides.

Alchemy of Snowflakes and Stars

Sprinkling snow like fairy dust,
Winter’s magic is a must.
With each flake a wish, the kids proclaim,
'Can we eat it? Or is that lame?'

Stars twinkle bright in the winter's night,
While snowmen argue who’s the best sight.
One claims to have a funnier grin,
The other just giggles, 'Let's try again!'

Frosty wonders make mischief thrive,
As children in boots take a joyful dive.
The crunch underfoot is pure delight,
A symphony of laughter in the moonlight.

From snowball cannons to icicle fights,
Every minute's packed with funny delights.
In this land of snow, we find our glee,
An alchemy of frosty jubilee!

The Art of Winter’s Embrace

With every flake, a canvas bright,
Winter laughs, painting day and night.
Kids tumble in snow like they’re on a spree,
While the dog just wants to be free!

Snowflakes whisper silly jokes,
As snowmen gather and proudly boast.
'How tall am I? Look at my hat!'
They all chuckle, 'We love this chat!'

The cold bites but we don’t care,
Wrapped in layers, we’re quite the pair.
With each hot cocoa, we toast to fun,
In this frosty realm, we’ve only begun!

So dance through the drifts, let out a cheer,
Embrace this winter, we hold dear.
For laughter's the warmth that fills the air,
In the art of winter, joy's everywhere!

In the Heart of Winter's Grasp

Snowflakes dance like they're on a spree,
While I trip over invisible debris.
My mittens are damp, but my spirits soar,
Sledding down hills, what could be more?

Everyone's hustling, bundled, and bold,
But I've lost a boot in the snowdrift's hold.
I shout for help, but it's all in jest,
As I wriggle and laugh, giving it my best.

Snowmen glisten, with noses of carrot,
I put on a scarf—that belongs to a ferret!
They just stare back, those frosty amigos,
While I boast of my antics and outrageous legos.

Oh, winter's here with a frosty cheer,
But I can't feel my toes, oh dear, oh dear!
With a hot chocolate splash and a silly grin,
Life's a snowball fight; let the fun begin!

When the World Wears White

The world has donned a fluffy white coat,
I stumble outside, all hope to gloat.
But look at my hair, it's all a-glitter,
Thanks to the snowball—oh, what a bitter!

Kids build forts, I'll join them in fun,
But my epic snowball hits—none have come.
I miss, I swerve, and crash in the snow,
While my laughter rings out in the winter glow.

Dogs dash past me, tails a-swish,
They frolic and play, fulfilling each wish.
I throw a snowflake, but it's more like mush,
Landing on a nose with quite a loud hush!

So here I sit in this snowy delight,
With runaway mittens that give quite a fright.
Yet in all the madness, I find pure bliss,
Is there a winter mishap I'd truly miss?

Chasing Shadows in a Glacial Light

I tiptoe through drifts, careful and sly,
Chasing my shadow as it waves goodbye.
The sun's feeble rays make ice dance around,
But my footing is shaky, oh what a sound!

I leap like a gazelle—or maybe a fish,
Making snow angels, that’s my winter wish.
But getting up’s tricky, I’m stuck to the ground,
Getting giggles from passers who think I’m profound.

Icicles glimmer like teeth in the night,
I ponder the physics—they give me a fright!
“Don’t slip!” my friends yell, while I twirl in my freeze,
I’m just creating my own winter breeze!

Amidst all this magic, I’ll take a quick spin,
With each frosty tumble, I’m crowned with a grin.
In a world all a-glimmer, I find my delight,
Chasing the shadows with all of my might.

Etched in Ice and Imagination

My yard transformed, it’s an ice skating rink,
But I check my balance and hesitate to think.
With a wobble and giggle, I make my first try,
I twirl like a reindeer who’s learning to fly!

The neighbor’s cat watches, with eyes wide and round,
As I glide and collide with each shimmery bound.
I give it my all, with flair and some grace,
But I land in a pile, so much for the race.

The frost gives a chuckle—I hear it quite clear,
As snowmen clap hands, they’ve risen in cheer.
I’ll carve my own destiny with dreams in the cold,
Each slip and each slide, a story retold.

There's magic in winter—a joy to embrace,
Even when landing takes up all of my space.
So bring on the laughter, the ice, and delight,
For each frozen moment is brilliantly bright!

Midnight’s Frostbitten Breath

On a chilly night we tread,
With noses red and cheer quite spread.
Snowball fights that leave us laughing,
While winter's breath keeps on drafting.

Socks are wet, and gloves are gone,
Yet still we dance until the dawn.
Frosty footprints, a silly trace,
In our hearts, we find our place.

Mittens stuck on every tree,
As if they chose to rebel with glee.
Snowflakes falling like confetti,
In this shivering, silly spree!

Hot cocoa spills with joy and cheer,
Laughter echoes, crystal clear.
We embrace the snowy mess,
Chasing joy, we won’t digress.

Beneath a Whispering Frost

The trees wear coats of crystal lace,
While squirrels strut at a funny pace.
They chatter loudly in surprise,
At frosty flakes that kiss the skies.

We slip and slide like clumsy bears,
The ground becomes a slide of snares.
With every thud and every fall,
Our giggles echo through it all.

A snowman dons a hat askew,
With carrots that are quite askew.
His stick arms wave in vain delight,
As we make snow angels, what a sight!

Frosty breath and silly grins,
In this world of white, fun begins.
Laughter dances through the air,
Beneath this frosty, whimsical layer.

Fragments of a Winter’s Muse

In winter's grip, we find our art,
With icy brushes, we play our part.
Snowflakes twirl like playful sprites,
Creating joy in frosty nights.

Carrots lost in a snowy heap,
As dreams of warmth make us leap.
With every slip and merry shout,
We capture fun, there's no doubt!

Polar bears in hats and ties,
Chasing snowflakes as the crow flies.
In this canvas of pure delight,
We paint the world with laughs so bright.

Every whimsy takes its flight,
Frosty acts, oh what a sight!
As giggles bounce from tree to tree,
In our winter's muse, we're wild and free.

Silver Hues on Nature's Palette

Nature's palette shines in white,
With silver hues in morning light.
Creatures prance with playful glee,
While snowflakes tickle, can't you see?

Pinecone hats on furry heads,
As we tumble into chilly beds.
Laughter echoes, crisp and clear,
As frosty friends draw near, oh dear!

Snow-covered fences, a gleaming line,
With cheerful hearts, we intertwine.
The world adorned in sparkling cheer,
As we bound through winter's sphere.

With rosy cheeks and snowball fights,
Our winter tales become highlights.
So here we are, in frosty air,
Creating joy, without a care.

Frost-Kissed Serenity

Chill in the air, oh what a delight,
Squirrels wearing jackets, quite the sight!
Snowflakes arguing, who's the best?
Dancing like they're on a frosty quest.

Mittens lost in the misty white flakes,
Did that snowman just join our takes?
With carrots for noses, they puff out their chests,
I think they're winning all the snowman contests!

Laughter erupts as the ice starts to crack,
Did that penguin just slip? I'll buy him a snack!
Penguins in tuxedos, what a quaint affair,
With snowballs and giggles, we float through the air.

Giggling gales swirl through the trees,
Barely held in by the perfect freeze.
Wintertime antics, what a grand show,
Everyone's smiling, even the snow!

Echoing Through the Crystal Pines

Whispers of laughter beneath the tall trees,
Owls in sweaters, enjoying the breeze.
The pinecones are rolling, playing hide and seek,
Who knew winter's fun could reach such a peak?

A snowball fight caused a ruckus so grand,
With innocent faces, no one has planned.
"Oh dear, my hat!" exclaims a young lad,
As the frost giants march, feeling quite rad.

Icicles hanging like teeth from the eaves,
A snowman debates if he wants to leave!
With a snowflake yawn, he stretches his arm,
And the humor supplies all the spirit and charm.

Echoes of joy bounce off frosted trees,
As cocoa and friends bring warmth like a breeze.
Every giggle that drifts through the night,
Turns winter's frigid into pure delight!

Twilight's Icy Embrace

The sun dips low, and all seems a blur,
While hedgehogs in goggles wait for the spur.
Hot cocoa spills, creating sweet trails,
As marshmallows dance like tiny white whales.

Chilly cheeks puffed, laughing together,
Ice skates on ponds, like birds of a feather.
The moon beams down with a cheeky grin,
And snowflakes chuckle, let the fun begin!

Twilight whispers, "Would you like to snuggle?"
But wait! Here comes the wild snowball struggle!
With a flurry of giggles and cheeks turning pink,
We dive into snowdrifts—to yell and to wink.

Stars twinkle gently, winks in the night,
As frost bites our toes, we bask in delight.
Right here in the cold, we find warmth in cheer,
As laughter resounds, filling all with good cheer!

Between Light and Glimmering Shadows

Between shadows that dance, the fun never stops,
Children are tumbling, doing wild hops.
Lights flashing bright like stars in a dream,
Snowflakes join in, it’s quite the team!

Rabbits in boots, bouncing away,
Frolicking through snowflakes, so merry and gay.
“Who’s got the carrot?” The snowmen all laugh,
As they gather around for a frosty old chaff.

Gloves flung high as the laughter drops low,
Shivers from giggles warm hearts in the snow.
Starlight above sparks joy like a dare,
Twirling and spinning, with frost in our hair.

Between the moonlight and chilly moon glow,
We twirl through the night, our spirits aglow.
The world is our playpen, laughter's the key,
In this glittering wonder, we are forever free!

Frostbitten Melodies of the Dark

A penguin slips on frozen ground,
With every flail, a goofy sound.
His dance is wild, his feathers askew,
Oh, what a sight! We laugh anew.

The snowflakes twirl like they own the night,
While snowmen grin with frosty delight.
A snowball fight breaks out in glee,
Not so snowy for the poor old tree!

Icicles drip like a frozen sneeze,
Making us giggle with the cold breeze.
Each mistletoe caught in a chilly embrace,
Where couples kiss, with a wintry face!

So here we are, in the cold’s sweet grip,
With laughter and cheer on this slippery trip.
Frosted laughs and a chilly cheer,
Winter's own comedy, perfectly clear!

Beneath the Icebound Canopy

Beneath the branches, icy and blue,
The rabbits play tag without much clue.
Each jump leads to a flip and a flop,
Leaving us in stitches, we can’t stop!

Under the trees wrapped up in white,
A squirrel shimmies, fearless, and bright.
But wait! What’s that? A slip, a slide,
The poor little guy has now lost his pride!

Frosty fun in a winter’s embrace,
With tumbleweeds made from snow, just in case.
An igloo built with a serious design,
Yet ends up looking like a twisted line!

So gather ‘round this quirky sight,
Where laughter echoes in the chilly night.
Under the icebound trees we play,
Winter's humor is here to stay!

Choreography of Crystalline Reflections

A snowflake twirls in a grand ballet,
Spinning and gliding, it winks on its way.
One tiny slip, it lands on my nose,
I laugh out loud, my giggle grows!

The frozen pond, a mirror so bright,
Reflects all the fun in the shimmering light.
We skate and spin in this crystal dance,
While juggling snowballs, we take our chance!

Snow angels flop with a frosty cheer,
While giggling seals peek out from near.
They join the fun in this frosty glow,
With silly moves that steal the show!

So grab your friends and let’s have a ball,
In this winter wonderland, we’ll never fall.
With crystalline laughter in every sway,
We dance till night steals the light away!

Dappled Light on Arctic Whispers

In dappled light, the shadows prance,
Polar bears join in on the dance.
With every step, they bump and glide,
All furry chaos, no need to hide!

The seals crack jokes, they're quite the crowd,
With punchlines loud and laughter proud.
An iceberg wobbles, a teetering show,
And down it goes – oh, no, oh, no!

The sun peeks through, all sparkly bright,
While penguins stumble, what a sight!
A comedy of errors on ice so slick,
Each slip and fall just adds to the trick!

So here's to winter, with joy and glee,
With giggles and wiggles, just let it be.
In the frosty air, where fun never quits,
Dappled laughter is where winter sits!

Milton Keynes UK
Ingram Content Group UK Ltd.
UKHW022341171124
451242UK00007B/82

9 789916 945025